A Painful History of Medicine

Pills, Powders & Potions
a history of medication

John Townsend

Chicago, Illinois

© 2006 Raintree
Published by Raintree,
A division of Reed Elsevier, Inc.
Chicago, Illinois

Customer Service 888–363–4266

Visit our website at www.raintreelibrary.com

Printed and bound in China by South China
Printing Company

10 09 08 07 06
10 9 8 7 6 5 4 3 2 1

Library of Congress Cataloging-in-
Publication Data
Townsend, John, 1955-
  Pills, powders & potions : a history of
medication / John Townsend.
     p.; cm. -- (Freestyle express) (A painful
history of medicine)
  Includes bibliographical references and index.
  ISBN 1-4109-2540-4 (hardback) -- ISBN 1-4109-
2545-5 (library binding)
  1. Drugs--History--Juvenile literature.
  2. Pharmacology--History--Juvenile literature.
  3. Therapeutics--History--Juvenile literature.
  I. Title. II. Title: Pills, powders and potions. III.
Series. IV. Series: Townsend, John, 1955- Painful
history of medicine
  RM301.17.T69 2006a
  615'.1--dc22
  2006009997

This leveled text is a version of *Freestyle: A Painful
History of Medicine: Pills, Powders and Potions*

Acknowledgments
Alamy Images pp. **9**, **18–19** (Kathleen
Watmough), **31** (Nigel Cattlin); Art Directors
and Trip p. **26**; A–Z Botanical Collection p. **18**;
Corbis pp. **6** (Keren Su), **7** (Paul A Souders), **10**
(Douglas P Wilson/ Frank Lane Picture Agency)
17 (Stapleton Collection), **24–25** (George D
Lepp), **27**, **28** (Bettmann), **32–33** (Randy Faris),
39 (Mario Beauregard), **43**, **45**, **46**, **48** (D Rober
& Lorri Franz), **48–49** (Craig Lovell), **50**
(Lawrence Manning); Alamy Images/ Dynamic
Graphics Group/ IT Stock Free p. **42**; Ginny
Stroud-Lewis pp. **4–5**, **23**, **25**, **30–31**, **33**, **38**;
Harcourt Education Ltd/ Tudor Photography p.
36; Mary Evans Picture Library p. **29**; Medical o
Line pp. **10–11**, **16**; Photodisc pp. **50–51**;
Ronald Grant Archive pp. **8–9**; Science Museum
Science & Society Picture Library pp. **19**, **20**,
20–21, **21**, **28**; Science Photo Library pp. **6–7**
(BSIP, Chassenet), **12–13**, **15**, **23** (Jean-Loup
Charmet), **30** (Andrew Syred), **32** (Th Foto-
Werbung), **34–35** (Joyce Photographics), **35**
(Cordelia Molloy), **37** (Hattie Young), **38–39**
(Edelmann), **40** (Dr P Marazzi), **40–41**
(Professors PM Motta & S Makabe), **41** (Scott
Camazine), **44** (Dept Of Medical Photography, S
Stephen's Hospital, London), **44–45** (John Cole
47 (CC Studio); The Advertising Archive p. **24**;
The Bridgeman Art Library/ Archives Charmet
p. **6**; The Ronald Grant Archive p. **14**; The
Wellcome Library, London pp. **8**, **22**; ZEFA/
stock4b/ Felbert & Gickenberg p. **13**.

Cover photograph of boy receiving injection
reproduced with permission of Popperfoto

The paper used to print this book comes from
sustainable resources.

Disclaimer
All the Internet addresses (URLs) given in this book
were valid at the time of going to press. However,
due to the dynamic nature of the Internet, some
addresses may have changed, or sites may have
changed or ceased to exist since publication. While
the author and publishers regret any inconvenience
this may cause readers, no responsibility for any
such changes can be accepted by either the author
or the publishers.

Contents

Any words appearing in the text in bold,
like this, are explained in the glossary.
You can also look out for them in the Word
bank at the bottom of each page.

Magic Pills

People take about 30 million pills every hour! We mix powders in water and drink them. We swallow **potions** from **medicine** bottles. We rub mixtures into our skin.

We hope these medicines will make us feel better. They could:

- take away pain
- cure illness
- stop us from becoming ill
- make us live longer.

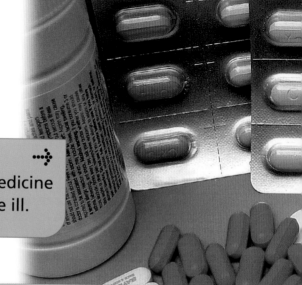

Most people today take medicine when they are ill.

Word bank   **potion**   liquid mixture that can be used as a medicine or a poison

Big money

Today medical drugs are worth a lot of money. Nearly all of us take them at some time in our lives.

Medicines were made from different parts of plants. Many medicines still have chemicals from plants in them.

It takes a long time to develop and test our medicines. They often work very well. But this was not always the case.

Find out later...

...which pill for headaches can also save lives.

...which Australian tree was used to make medicines.

...which potion uses chopped cockroach.

medicine   substance used to treat an illness

Ancient Times

Ancient people lived thousands of years ago. They worked hard to find **cures** for illness.

They tried and tested many plants. First they would grind them up. They used a **mortar** and pestle (below) to do this. Then they soaked or boiled the powder. The new **medicine** had to be tried. That was risky. It could kill or cure them.

Dried lizards were used in Chinese medicines.

China

Shen Nung was a Chinese emperor. He probably lived about 4,500 years ago. He is remembered for testing hundreds of herbs on himself.

Word bank **cure** something that heals or makes an illness better

Egypt

The Egyptians lived around 4,000 years ago. They made all kinds of medicines. In some cases they used honey as an **antiseptic**. This stopped some diseases spreading.

The Egyptians did not know what caused diseases. Sometimes their medicines did not work. Then they prayed to gods and spirits.

Australia

Some **Aboriginal Australians** crush the leaves of the eucalyptus tree (below). The strong smell can clear the nose, throat, and lungs.

The father of medicine

Hippocrates was a Greek doctor. He is known as the "father of **medicine**." His ideas are used in medicine today.

Hippocrates found out many things. He worked out how some drugs acted on the body. Wine and **opium** are drugs. Hippocrates also knew about deadly plants. **Mandrake** (left) is a deadly plant.

Harvesting mandrake

It is tricky getting mandrake roots out of the ground. You cannot grip them because you would get poison on your hands. The Greeks used ropes to pull them up.

A sip of mandrake helped to ease the pain of crucifixion.

Word bank

opium drug made from opium poppies. It relaxes people and helps ease pain.

Mandrake

The mandrake root can kill you. Mandrake is a **poison**.

The Romans made mandrake into a "death-wine." They gave it to people who were being **crucified**. The mandrake put them to sleep until they died. It helped ease their pain.

Bald

People have always tried to cure baldness. Mostly they rubbed things on their heads to make their hair grow.

- Hippocrates used pigeon droppings.

- Aristotle, the Greek teacher, tried goats' **urine**.

crucify   nail someone to a wooden cross

Romans

The Romans had a big effect on **medicine**. Their cities had many healers. There were doctors, teachers, and "wise women." They sold many medicines.

Galen was a famous doctor in Roman times. He had one mixture that he used to treat patients. It was supposed to be a **cure** for most illnesses. It had 77 **ingredients** in it.

Healing plants

St. John's wort (above) is a plant used in creams and oils. It helps heal sore skin. It has been found growing at the sites of Roman villages.

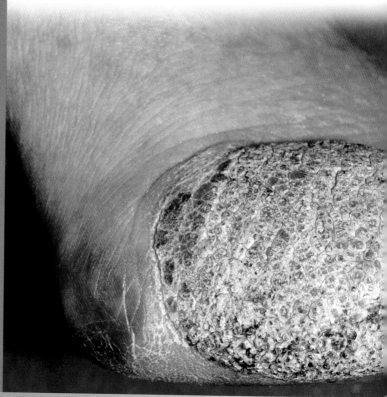

Word bank   ointment   oily substance rubbed on to skin to help heal it

Roman cures

The Romans used all kinds of **ointments**. The Romans put these on to the skin. They did this to clean wounds and sores. One ointment was made from a white powder, called **arsenic**. Arsenic is a deadly **poison**!

The Romans rubbed garlic onto battle wounds. This was smelly. It helped to heal them. This is because garlic juice kills germs. It is a **disinfectant**.

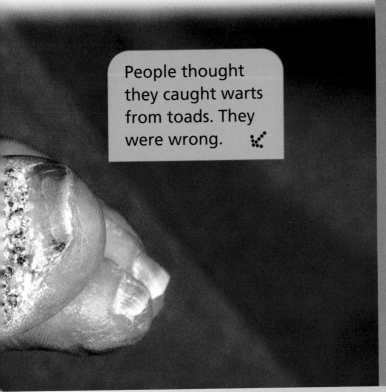

People thought they caught warts from toads. They were wrong.

The Middle Ages

The **Middle Ages** was a time in European history. It was 500 to 1,500 years ago. There were lots of new ideas about **medicine** then. Many ideas came from **Muslim** countries. These countries are where people follow **Islam**. Islam is a religion. Islam teaches people how to care for the body.

At that time Muslim medicine was the best in the world.

An Arab doctor is ⋯➤ making a medicine. He will use it to treat snake bites.

Word bank   **Middle Ages**   period of European history; roughly between AD 500 and 1500

Muslim medicine

Muslim doctors had many new ideas about medicine. They used herbs in different ways. They made new drugs.

One new idea was to boil plants in water. Patients then breathed in, or **inhaled**, the steam. This helped them to breathe. It is a treatment still used today. If an idea worked, it was written down. This was then passed on to others.

Yuck!

Muslim doctors tried to make medicines taste better. They added rose water and orange blossom.

But not all of their medicines were nice. One was made of leaves boiled in camel's **urine**. Yuck!

Islam   religion of Muslims, who follow the teachings of Muhammad

Monks

The **Muslim** faith grew in the **Middle Ages**. But it was not the only religion that did this. The **Christian** church spread, too. **Monasteries** were built across Europe. **Monks** lived, studied, and looked after the sick in monasteries.

Monks grew plants in their gardens. They collected them from woods and fields. Monks boiled up the plants (below). They tested the juices on patients. If the juices worked, the monks wrote down the **recipes**.

Word bank   Christian   follower of Jesus Christ and his teachings

Making a link

Monks tried to make links between some illnesses and plants:

A walnut looks like a brain. Try using it for headaches.

Jaundice is a disease that makes the skin turn yellow. Try using yellow plants.

But these treatments did not work. It was time to use science to find **cures**.

Not much good

Terrible **plagues** hit Europe in the Middle Ages. Plagues are deadly diseases. They spread very quickly. Monks tried to find cures. But most cures did no good at all.

Monks cared for plague victims.

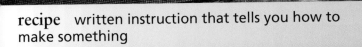

recipe   written instruction that tells you how to make something

15

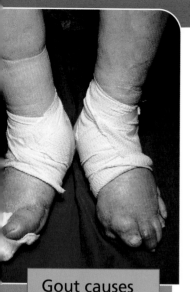

Doctors

What would you do if you were ill in the **Middle Ages**? Many villages had a wise woman or witch. You could go and see her. She used old beliefs and stories to treat illness.

There were other people who could treat you. You could pay to see a doctor or a **monk**. Many towns also had their own chemist shop.

Cure for gout

"Put the frog's right leg on the right foot and the left leg on the left foot."

*This **cure** is for **gout**. It is from the 11th century.*

Inside a chemist shop in 1751. ✝

Word bank

monk   man who is a member of a religious community

Chemists

Chemist shops in the 13th century were lined with shelves (below). They were filled with jars, bottles, and **mortars**. Plants and other materials are ground up in a mortar with a tool called a pestle.

All pills were made by hand. To make pills, chemists would coat their hands in oil. Then they rolled the pills between their hands. The pills were left to dry and harden.

Molasses

Molasses was supposed to be a wonder drug. It was said to help the stomach and heal wounds. It could help people sleep. It was even said to cure the **plague**. Probably it just tasted nice!

plague   deadly disease that spreads quickly

Good for Business

Sick people will pay a lot of money to feel better. But often they do not know if they are spending their money wisely.

Trial and error

Doctors often did not know if a treatment worked or not. Some doctors tried out new mixtures on their patients. Some **medicines** were made from things like spiderwebs, earthworms, and woodlice. They were horrible!

Poison

Pharmacists study and make drugs. French pharmacists made **strychnine** from the dog button plant (below). Strychnine is a **poison**, and it can kill. But in tiny doses, it was used to help the **appetite**.

Word bank   appetite   eating well

Tobacco

In the 1700s **tobacco** was used widely. Many people thought it could **cure** anything. No one knew how bad tobacco was for you.

Nicolas Monardes was a Spanish doctor. He used tobacco to treat many problems. He used it to treat toothache and joint pains. Many people chewed tobacco. Some did this to avoid getting the **plague**.

John Bell's chemist shop in London.

Tobacco leaves, like this, were once used to cure diseases.

Open all hours

John Bell opened a pharmacy in 1798. He sold pills, powders, and liquids, called **potions**. Rich people bought them. The shop opened at 7 A.M. and closed at 11 P.M. It made a lot of money.

tobacco dried leaves of a plant used for smoking or chewing

Quack doctors

At one time anyone could be a doctor. Many doctors knew some **medicine**. Others were cheats. These were called quack doctors.

In the 1700s there were a lot of quack doctors. They sold medicines that did not work. But people believed the quacks. They used their worthless medicines.

This is a quack. They talked very quickly to get people to buy.

Did you know?

"Quack" comes from the word "quacksalver." This was someone who sold healing **remedies**, like **salves**.

Word bank   **salve**   healing or soothing ointment

False medicines

Quack doctors said their medicines did all sorts of things. They were telling lies. There were no laws to stop quack doctors from lying.

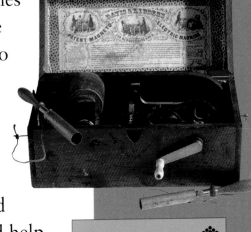

James Graham was a quack doctor in the late 1700s. He treated people in London. They paid a lot of money to be bathed in mud. Graham said this would help them live longer.

This electrical machine was supposed to **cure** illness.

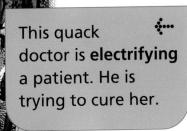

This quack doctor is **electrifying** a patient. He is trying to cure her.

End of the quacks

Quack doctors disappeared in the 1800s. New laws were passed to stop quacks from selling false medicines.

electrify   pass electricity through something

Success story

Dropsy was a common disease in the 1700s. It made people swell up like a balloon. Their lungs got squashed. They could not breathe.

William Withering was a doctor. In 1775 he had a patient dying from dropsy. Withering could not help. So the patient got a **remedy** from a gypsy. In a few days, he got better. The gypsy told Withering the main **ingredient** in her remedy. It was a foxglove flower.

Life and death

Digitalis is still used as a drug. It helps some types of heart disease. But it has to be taken in small amounts. It is a **poison** and can kill.

Dropsy used to be a big problem.

Word bank

remedy medicine or treatment that should make an illness better

Heart disease

The foxglove (below) contains a chemical. It is called **digitalis**. Digitalis can be deadly. Even so, Withering tried it out on his patients.

Doctor Withering thought dropsy might be linked to heart disease. He gave his heart patients dried foxglove leaves. This got their hearts going. It also cured their dropsy. This was a big discovery.

Dropsy and consumption

This picture above shows **Consumption** (the skinny woman) and Dropsy (the swollen man). Dropsy was a common disease 300 years ago. Dr Withering used foxglove (left) to cure dropsy.

consumption   disease that causes fever and lung failure. It is also called tuberculosis.

In the 1800s people began to travel farther. They visited places they had not been to before. In these places they found all sorts of different treatments.

Old home remedies

Many **remedies** were homemade. They used **ingredients** from the kitchen. Some of these were:

- hot water and pepper for an upset stomach
- castor oil as a **laxative**. This means it helps you go to the toilet.

Slime

"Cover snails in brown sugar. Wrap them in a clean cloth. Hang the cloth over a bowl. Let the juice drip into it. Drink the liquid."

*Old British **cure** for a sore throat.*

Brown sugar and snail slime— just right for a sore throat!

Word bank

asthma   disease that affects the lungs, making it difficult to breathe

United States

In the 1800s many parts of the United States were a long way from towns. They were **remote**. There were few doctors. Most mothers made home **medicines**. Then they could treat their families themselves.

For a chest cold, spread on goose grease. For sprained joints mix apple vinegar with an egg white.

A cure for **athlete's foot** was to stand in a cowpie!

athlete's foot   itchy infection of fungus between the toes

In the wars

In 1861 the American **Civil War** started. The people from the north of the country began to fight the people in the south.

There were many battles. Thousands of soldiers were badly hurt. They were taken to **field hospitals**. But there were never enough **medicines** to go round. The doctors found plants growing nearby. Doctors used these to make medicines.

Progress

Wars helped make medicine better. Doctors had to try new drugs because so many people were sick and injured. They had to find out how the drugs worked.

Doctors learned a lot in the American Civil War.

Word bank

field hospital hospital near a battlefield, often in a tent

Treating wounds

Gunshot wounds were a big problem in the Civil War. They often got badly **infected**. The flesh began to rot. When this happens it is called **gangrene**. The doctors had to stop the gangrene. They cut off patients' arms and legs. But often the gangrene came back to the stump. The doctors needed medicines to treat the **infections**.

Making medicines

In the Civil War, many soldiers had problems going to the toilet. This was because of the poor food. To help this, doctors made **laxatives**. One doctor gave men strong tea. It was made from peach leaves and hot **lard** mixed with syrup.

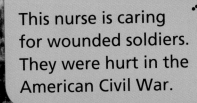

This nurse is caring for wounded soldiers. They were hurt in the American Civil War.

infection   illness or disease caused by living things growing in the body

27

Big business

Lydia Pinkham was a housewife. She was from Massachusetts. For years she made a **tonic** for her family. Tonics are **medicines** that make you feel better. This one was made from herbs and alcohol.

In 1873 she began to sell her tonic. She said it cured **cramps**. She also claimed it stopped women getting dizzy. Lydia died a very rich woman!

Medicine jokes

The cartoon above is from 1834. It is making fun of some pills. The man on the left has a pair of false legs under his arm. He has grown a new pair of legs!

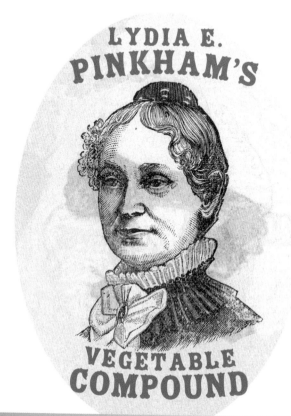

LYDIA E. PINKHAM'S

VEGETABLE COMPOUND

Word bank   tonic   type of medicine that makes you feel better

Snake-oil salesman

John Meyer was a salesman. In the 1880s he traveled around the United States. Native Americans told him about a type of plant root. This had healing powers. Meyer made it into a juice. Then he sold it in bottles. He said it would **cure** many things. He even let a snake bite him. This was to prove his cure worked. The root used by Meyer was echinacea.

Wind pills were around in 1870. They were supposed to cure **flatulence**.

Worms

Some types of worm live inside our bodies. Tapeworms do this.

We can catch tapeworms from our food and water. Tapeworms lay eggs. These pass out of our body in our waste. Animals can eat them. They can get them on their fur. If we eat meat from these animals or touch them, the eggs can get inside us. The eggs grow into more worms. We should cook meat properly and wash our hands before we eat.

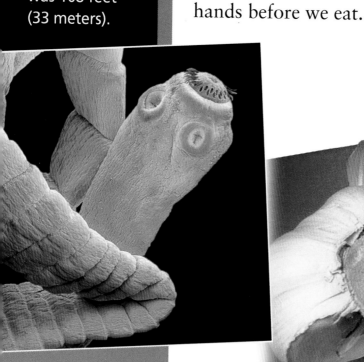

Word bank   cure   something that heals or makes an illness better

Old remedy

Having worms makes you ill. One old treatment was to starve the patient for three days. Hot soup was held to the patient's mouth. People thought the worm would come out of the mouth. It would want to feed on the soup because it was hungry. Then they would grab it. This never worked!

Today there are drugs to deal with worms.

People think that garlic and onions are good for the health. ⋖⋯

Cockroaches

In Asia some people think that cockroaches (above) are a **cure** for illnesses. Many people believe they help fight colds. Some people even eat them to live longer!

Wonder Drugs

Some drugs have helped the health of millions of people.

Special acid

People have chewed white willow bark. This has eased pain for a long time.

In England in 1758, Edward Stone chewed some white willow bark. It helped fever and toothache. He was so pleased that he told some scientists. They found acid was in the bark. It was the painkiller.

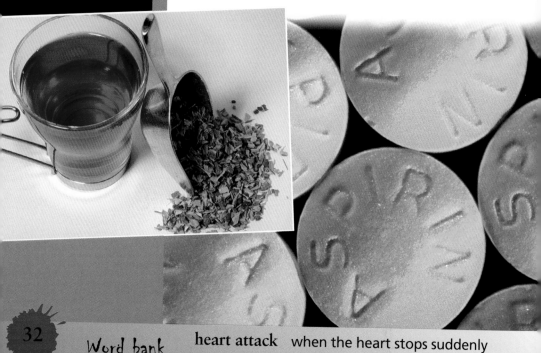

Word bank   **heart attack**   when the heart stops suddenly

Aspirin

White willow bark was a good painkiller. But it was not very good to take. Scientists needed to turn it into a proper drug.

German scientist Felix Hoffmann did this. In 1897 he made a chemical based on the acid. The new chemical was called aspirin. In 1915 the first aspirin pills were made.

Aspirin pills can be taken whole or in water.

Lifesaver

Aspirin is a painkiller. It is good for headaches. It also stops **heart attacks** and **strokes**. Aspirin saves many lives each year this way.

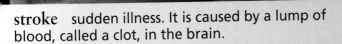

stroke sudden illness. It is caused by a lump of blood, called a clot, in the brain.

Penicillin

In 1928 **penicillin** was found. It was the first **antibiotic**. This means it kills harmful **bacteria**. Bacteria are tiny living things that can cause disease.

British scientist Alexander Fleming discovered penicillin. The penicillin was growing in a dish of bacteria. He saw how it killed the bacteria.

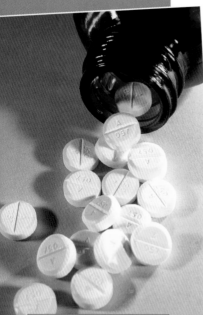

These penicillin pills are lifesavers.

Did you know?

Over 110 million pounds (50 million kilograms) of penicillin are made each year.

Word bank   antibiotic   drug that kills harmful bacteria

Early days

Scientists tested penicillin. They found that it helped the body fight disease.

Until the 1940s many people died from wounds. They turned **septic**. This means that harmful bacteria grew in the wounds. The bacteria **poisoned** their blood. Penicillin helped to stop this. Penicillin is now used all over the world.

Superbugs

Antibiotics have helped to save many lives. But some bacteria are not killed by them. They are called superbugs. Scientists have to make new antibiotics to kill the superbugs.

This is penicillin mold. It is growing on a tangerine.

septic   infected with bacteria

Mystery disease

Diabetes can make people very ill. For years it puzzled doctors. People with diabetes lost weight. This happened even if they ate a lot. In the end the disease would kill them. People with diabetes lost sugar in their **urine**.

Sugar loss

Our bodies need sugar for energy. But people with diabetes lose their sugar. This makes them feel very tired. They can also have skin and eye problems.

Sweet urine is a sign of diabetes.

Word bank

urine   waste liquid passed from the body, usually pale yellow

Diabetes

People have diabetes because their bodies do not make enough **insulin**. Insulin is a chemical. It is made in the **pancreas**. It helps us use sugar. Insulin moves sugar from the blood into the body's **cells**.

People with diabetes have to inject insulin into their blood. The insulin then controls their sugar levels.

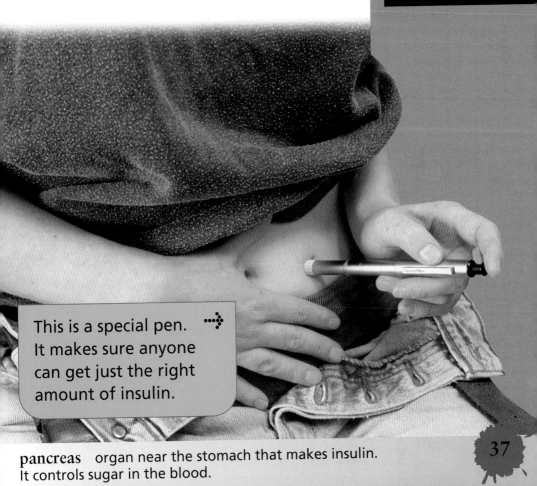

This is a special pen. It makes sure anyone can get just the right amount of insulin.

pancreas   organ near the stomach that makes insulin. It controls sugar in the blood.

37

Modern Times

In the last 50 years, many new **medicines** have been made. Some are amazing. They have helped sick people become well. Some were a disaster.

A drug called thalidomide was like this. It first came out in 1956. It helped pregnant women who felt sick. But it was not tested properly. It damaged unborn babies. Many babies were born without arms and legs.

Danger

Drugs are always risky. Some people react badly to certain drugs. They have an **allergy** to the drug. You must be careful when you take any medicine.

An unborn baby in the womb at seven weeks.

Word bank   **allergy**   when you have a bad reaction to something

Risk

Thalidomide was used for five years. Some women took it only once. Even then it caused harm. About 12,000 children were born without arms and legs. In 1962 the drug was **banned**.

Thalidomide is being used again. But pregnant women are not using it. People take it to treat some skin problems. It has to be used with great care.

Big question

Today drugs have lots of tests before people use them. This is because of the thalidomide disaster. Often the drugs are tried out on animals first. Many people think this is wrong.

Many drugs are tested on animals. What do you think about this?

banned   not allowed

Cancer drugs

Cancer is a disease. Even today many people fear it. It happens when body **cells** begin to grow out of control. Cells are tiny units. They make up all plants and animals.

Cancer cells often form a growth or swelling. This is called a **tumor**. Cancer cells can spread to other parts of the body.

Too much sunbathing can cause skin cancer.

The battle goes on

Cancer is still a serious illness. But in the last few years, things have got better. Not as many people die from cancer as they used to.

This photo shows an ovary. There are cancer cells growing in it.

Word bank   cell   tiny unit that makes up all plant and animal tissue

Hope

Taxol is a drug that fights cancer. It is made from the bark of the Pacific yew tree. It is used to treat cancer of the **ovaries**. Taxol has saved the lives of many women.

There was a problem with Taxol. Each patient needed six whole, 100-year-old trees to make the drug. There were not enough trees. Luckily, other types of yew tree have chemicals nearly the same. Scientists now use these.

Drugs from plants

The plant below is a Madagascan periwinkle. It grows in the rainforest. It contains many chemicals. Two of them can kill cancer cells in the blood.

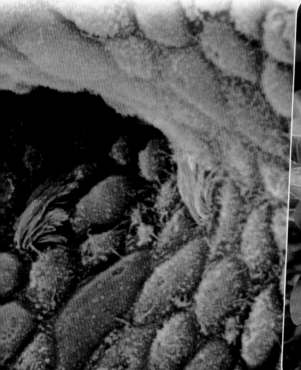

ovary   female organ that produces eggs

Treating the mind

Millions of people get **depressed**. Life can be miserable for them. Depression is an illness. It affects how people think. It changes their moods and feelings. It changes how they act. There are special chemicals in the brain. Sometimes these chemicals get out of balance. Then people can get depressed.

Feeling good

Serotonin is a chemical. It is made in the brain. It makes you feel good. Exercise helps the brain make more of it. That is why you feel good after exercise.

Exercise is good for the mind and the body.

Word bank   stress feeling under too much pressure

Pill-popping

There are now many drugs to treat the mind. These have come out in the second half of the 1900s.

- 1950s – Lithium was the first drug to help depression.
- 1963 – Valium was given to help **stress**. Many people could not stop taking it. They became **addicted**.
- 1987 – Prozac was a new drug to help depression. By 2000, 40 million people had taken Prozac.

Good mood food

If you eat a banana, it may cheer you up. Bananas help the body to make serotonin. This is the "feel good" chemical. Bananas are the only fruit that do this.

Some drugs help the brain to make more serotonin. This helps depression.

addicted   finding it difficult to manage without a certain drug

HIV and AIDS

There was a new disease in the early 1980s. A type of **virus** called HIV caused it. A virus is a type of tiny living thing. It can get inside **cells**. HIV is passed from person to person through body liquids. Blood and **semen** are body liquids.

If you have the HIV virus, you may then get **AIDS**. Then your body is unable to fight **infections**.

This AIDS patient has Kaposi's sarcoma. It is a type of cancer. People with HIV/AIDS often get this.

Word bank   **virus** tiny living thing that breaks into the body's cells and can cause disease

The search carries on

Some drugs slow down the effects of AIDS. But they are not a **cure**.

Most AIDS drugs work by stopping viruses from getting into the body. But the drugs cause **side effects**. Rashes and headaches are some of the side effects.

There is a new drug called Reverset. It has fewer side effects. Other new drugs are being made and tested.

This is the AIDS symbol. It is known all over the world.

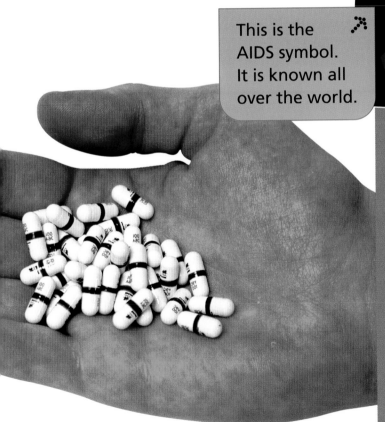

Major problem

The drugs used to treat AIDS (left) cost a lot of money. People in poor countries cannot afford them. Most people with AIDS live in poor countries.

semen fluid that contains sperm

Big changes

At one time drugs were only swallowed. They were taken as pills, powders, or **potions**. Here are some ways we take them today:

- A shot from a **vaccine** gun injects a known amount or dose. It gets into the body quickly.
- Skin patches are stuck on to the body. They pass drugs slowly into the blood.
- People with **asthma** can quickly "puff" on an **inhaler**.

Getting drugs

You can buy medical drugs at any time. Supermarkets are open all day. You can even buy **medicines** online.

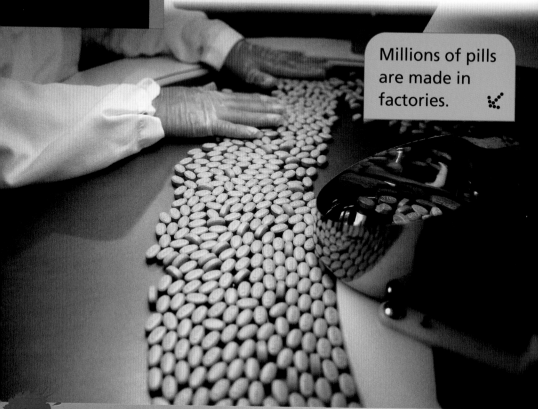

Millions of pills are made in factories.

Word bank

vaccine   medicine to make the body defend itself against a disease

Drugs in the United States

Medical drugs have always been worth a lot of money. But now they are worth more than ever.

- Doctors give out over three **billion** drugs in the United States each year.
- Drug companies advertise drugs. They spend over $3 billion a year on advertising.
- Each year 8.5 million Americans buy drugs. Many of the sales are because of advertising.

Back to plants

There are hundreds of different types of drugs now. But some people prefer not to use them at all. They would rather use the natural drugs found in plants.

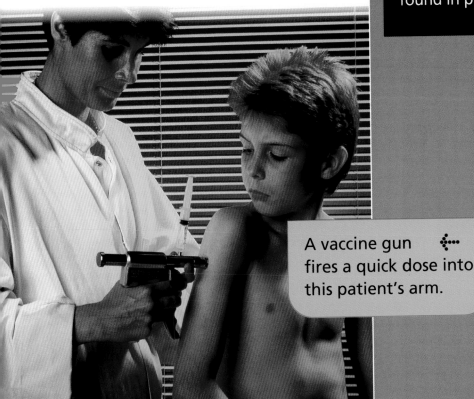

A vaccine gun fires a quick dose into this patient's arm.

---

billion   a thousand million

New drug

Scientists have found a new drug. It makes fat mice thin. The next test will be on baboons (below). This is because baboons put on weight in the same way as humans. This drug may help people who are very overweight.

In the news

There are lots of medical stories in the news. Here are some of the recent stories.

VICTIM LOSES SKIN

A woman from California lost all her skin. Sarah Teargain took an **antibiotic**, and all her skin peeled away. Even the skin in her mouth, throat, and eyes came away. Doctors thought she would die.

Doctors covered up her body with a man-made skin. They also gave her drugs. These stopped the bleeding.

Her own skin is now growing back. It is an amazing recovery.

Word bank   **antibiotic**   drug that kills harmful bacteria

A change of address!

Luis Manon lived in Cuzco, Peru. This is 11,025 feet (3,360 meters) above sea level. There is little oxygen in the air at this height. Luis was always tired. His heart had not grown properly. He needed more oxygen or an operation.

His family moved to Brazil. Brazil is much closer to sea level. There was more oxygen in the air. Luis felt fine. He didn't need heart surgery or drugs. He just needed a new address.

Licorice

Licorice is a plant root. It contains many drugs. One of these drugs could be used to help memory. Tests show it works on old people with memory problems. They just have to remember to take it!

Cuzco is in the mountains of Peru.

liquorice   type of plant root

Some people think that laughter is the best medicine.

And finally ...

It is the 21st century. But some medical claims still seem too amazing to be true.

Would you believe it?

In 2004 there were some special pantyhose. These were being sold in Austria. The makers said the pantyhose helped women lose weight. The nylons had **caffeine** in them. This is a drug found in tea and coffee. The new range of pantyhose soon sold out!

Laughter – the best medicine

In Brazil patients are trying a new treatment. They are given "laughter classes." These people have **depression**, **stress**, and **diabetes**. They all have to laugh out loud together.

Word bank   caffeine   drug found in coffee and tea

The future

Pills, powders, and **potions** have been in our lives for thousands of years. We take them to **cure** illness. We take them to feel or look good, and to live for a long time.

Soon we may find a cure for **AIDS** and cancer. A simple pill may stop us growing old. We could all look young and live for ever!

Old wives' tales

We are learning more about medicine. So a belief like the one below will become a thing of the past.

- Eating junk food gives you pimples 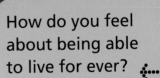 FALSE

Dead skin **cells**, **hormones**, and **bacteria** cause pimples.

How do you feel about being able to live for ever?

Find Out More

Books

Elliott, Lynne. *Medieval Medicine and the Plague: Medieval World*. New York: Crabtree Children's Books, 2006.

Parker, Steve. *Groundbreakers: Alexander Fleming*. Chicago: Heinemann Library, 2001.

Shuter, Jane. *A Century of Change: Health and Medicine*. Chicago: Heinemann Library, 2000.

Using the Internet

The Internet can tell you more about medicine through the ages. You can use a search engine, such as www.yahooligans.com.
Type in keywords such as:

- bacteria
- disinfectant
- Alexander Fleming + penicillin

Search tips

There are billions of pages on the Internet. It can be difficult to find what you are looking for.

These search tips will help you find useful websites more quickly:

- Know exactly what you want to find out about.
- Use two to six keywords in a search. Put the most important word first.
- Only use names of people, places, or things.

Where to search

Search engine
A search engine looks through millions of website pages. It lists all the sites that match the words in the search box. You will find the best matches are at the top of the list, on the first page.

Search directory
A person instead of a computer has sorted a search directory. You can search by keyword or subject and browse through the different sites. It is like looking through books on a library shelf.

Glossary

Aboriginal Australian native Australian

addicted finding it difficult to manage without a certain drug

AIDS Acquired Immune Deficiency Syndrome, a condition caused by the HIV virus

allergy when you have a bad reaction to something

antibiotic drug that kills harmful bacteria

antiseptic substance that stops harmful bacteria from growing. It also stops disease spreading.

appetite eating well

arsenic white powder that is a poison

asthma disease that affects the lungs, making it difficult to breathe

athlete's foot itchy infection of fungus between the toes

bacteria tiny living things that can cause illness or diease

billion a thousand million

caffeine drug found in coffee and tea

cell tiny unit that makes up all plant and animal tissue

Christian follower of Jesus Christ and his teachings

civil war when soldiers from the same country fight each other

consumption disease that causes fever and lung failure. It is also called tuberculosis.

cramp when your muscles seize up and hurt

crucify nail someone to a wooden cross

cure something that heals or makes an illness better

depressed feeling very down, upset, and unhappy

diabetes illness caused by the body not making enough insulin

digitalis drug used to treat the heart. It is from the foxglove plant.

disinfectant chemical that destroys germs

dropsy illness that causes water to collect in the body, often resulting in death

electrify pass electricity through something

field hospital hospital near a battlefield, often in a tent

flatulence body gas

gangrene when flesh rots and dies, due to infection or lack of blood

gout painful swelling of the toes

heart attack when the heart stops suddenly

hormone chemical inside the body

infect when living things grow inside or on the body and cause diseases

infection illness or disease caused by living things growing in the body

ingredient something that goes into a mixture or recipe

inhale breathe in

inhaler "puffer" device for breathing in a drug

insulin chemical inside the body that helps sugar move from the blood into the body cells

Islam religion of Muslims, who follow the teachings of Muhammad

lard hard fat from animals

laxative something that makes you need the toilet soon after taking it

licorice type of plant root

mandrake poisonous plant; the root was used as a drug

medicine substance used to treat an illness

Middle Ages period of European history; roughly between AD 500 and 1500

monastery place where monks live

monk man who is a member of a religious community

mortar pot where material is pounded with a tool called a pestle

Muslim follower of the prophet Muhammad

ointment oily substance rubbed on to skin to help heal it

opium drug made from opium poppies. It relaxes people and helps ease pain.

ovary female organ that produces eggs

pancreas organ near the stomach that makes insulin. It controls sugar in the blood.

penicillin first type of antibiotic made

pharmacist person who studies and makes medical drugs

plague deadly disease that spreads quickly

poison substance that can kill you, or the use of that substance to kill

potion liquid mixture that can be used as a medicine or a poison

recipe written instruction that tells you how to make something

remedy medicine or treatment that should make an illness better

remote long way from towns

salve healing or soothing ointment

semen fluid that contains sperm

septic infected with bacteria

serotonin chemical in the brain that helps you feel happy

side effect other problem a drug may cause

stress feeling under too much pressure

stroke sudden illness. It is caused by a lump of blood, called a clot, in the brain.

strychnine poisonous powder

tobacco dried leaves of a plant used for smoking or chewing

tonic type of medicine that makes you feel better

tumor swelling or growth of cells in the body that is not normal

urine waste liquid passed from the body, usually pale yellow

vaccine medicine to make the body defend itself against a disease

virus tiny living thing that breaks into the body's cells and can cause disease

Index